JUL 1 5

HISTORY'S GREATEST WARRIORS

NINJAS

MASTERS OF STEALTH
AND SECRECY

Patricia Dawson

Cavendish
Square

New York

Published in 2015 by Cavendish Square Publishing, LLC
243 5th Avenue, Suite 136, New York, NY 10016

Copyright © 2015 by Cavendish Square Publishing, LLC

First Edition

Library of Congress Cataloging-in-Publication Data

Dawson, Patricia (Patricia Adelaide)
Ninjas : masters of stealth and secrecy / Patricia Dawson.
pages cm. — (History's greatest warriors)
Includes index.
ISBN 978-1-50260-122-3 (hardcover) ISBN 978-1-50260-124-7 (ebook)
1. Ninja—Juvenile literature. I. Title.

UB271.J3D39 2015
355.5'48—dc23

2014026746

Editor: Amy Hayes
Copy Editor: Cynthia Roby
Art Director: Jeffrey Talbot
Designer: Joseph Macri
Senior Production Manager: Jennifer Ryder-Talbot
Production Editor: David McNamara
Photo Researcher: J8 Media

Printed in the United States of America

CONTENTS

INTRODUCTION

Jinichi Kawakami describes the uses of weapons displayed at the Iga Ninja Museum.

He is deadly with a two-inch blade, able to cut a rival's throat from a distance of twenty feet. He can mix a variety of chemicals to cause explosions, and has the ability to disappear in a cloud of smoke. He is the twenty-first head of the 500-year-old Ban clan of **ninjas**, but he may be destined to be the last. At 63, Jinichi Kawakami has decided to take the ancient art and skills of the traditional ninja with him to the grave, feeling there is no place for the ninja in modern society.

He was trained from the age of six in weapons, psychology, endurance, and more. He became the leader of the clan at the age of nineteen, and received the clan's ancient scrolls and traditional weapons. While he has been head of the clan for close to half a century, Kawakami now uses his ninja skills as the head of the Iga-ryu ninja museum. He is also doing research on the rich history of ninjas at Japan's Mie University.

Ninjas (also known as *Shinobi*) were key in shaping Japan's history for centuries. Over the years their legend has continued to grow, with people ascribing even more amazing and mystical powers to these ancient warriors. Today it is difficult to separate the history from the fiction, but both are fascinating in their own ways.

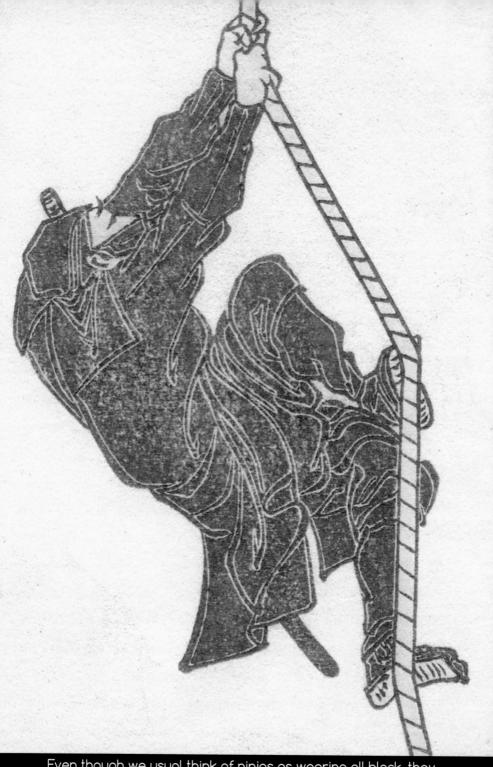

Even though we usual think of ninjas as wearing all black, they only wore black at night to blend in with their dark surroundings.

CHAPTER ONE

THE EARLIEST APPEARANCES OF NINJAS

Ninjas are everywhere in popular culture today, appearing in movies, comic books, and video games. They are often depicted using their **lethal** skills in **martial arts** with incredible weapons. Ninjas had impressive fighting skills, and they were also well trained in **stealth**. They became famous for dressing in black. However, they only dressed in black during the night. Throughout the day, they were more likely to be disguised as a merchant or monk.

Ninjas had many abilities that made them seem magical. However, it was their intense training that created this impression. Most people living during the

7

time of the ninja feared what they did not understand. They made up stories about ninjas having magical powers. Ninjas were happy to let these stories spread. It made them appear more threatening to their enemies.

The First Appearance of Ninjas

Ninjas were active in Japan from around the 1100s to the 1600s. During this time, Japan was ruled by a military leader called a **shogun**. The shogun used warlords to help him control Japan. Each warlord owned land. The warlords were constantly at war with each other to gain more power and land.

To protect them from enemy attacks, warlords used warriors called **samurai**. The warlords gave samurai land as payment for their loyalty and protection. This system of giving land in return for work, protection, and loyalty was known as **feudalism**.

The samurai followed a special code of honor. This code prevented them from

Samurai were the knights of Japan. They wore heavy armor and had a strict code of honor.

spying or doing other things that were thought to be dishonorable. However, the samurai were not the only group of warriors in Japan at this time. The other group lived by no such code. They simply did what their masters asked of them. These were the ninjas.

Iga and Koga

No one is exactly certain when ninjas first appeared. Most researchers agree that the birthplace of the ninja is the island of Honshu. Honshu is the largest of the four main islands that make up Japan. Iga and Koga were the places on Honshu where the first ninjas began to practice their secret skills.

The beautiful Iga Ueno castle is located in Iga, on Honshu. Iga was one of the first places where ninjas appeared.

Iga and Koga were melting pots of different cultures and ideas. During the fourth and fifth centuries, China had undergone political disorder. Many people left China during this time and settled in Iga and Koga. Among those who came to Honshu were monks and military leaders.

These newcomers shared their Chinese philosophies and fighting skills with their new neighbors. The Chinese were exposed to the ways of Honshu as well. The **techniques** and way of life of the ninjas grew out of this combining of skills and ideas.

The Shugenja

Many people who lived in Iga and Koga believed in the power of nature. They thought that humans could tap into the natural energy of the land. This was believed to make them physically and spiritually stronger. They also believed that people could learn to survive better in their world by understanding their physical surroundings.

A man walks of hot coals, a trial that many ninjas faced in order to become more powerful.

One group of people who believed in the power of nature was called the Shugenja. They repeatedly put themselves in dangerous situations. They thought this would help them overcome their personal fears and take on the powers of nature. Walking through fire was one of the dangers the Shugenja put themselves through. Many historians believe that early ninjas incorporated some of the Shugenja beliefs in their training.

The Rise of the Ninjas

Because ninjas followed a different ethical code than samurai, and practiced a different faith than the Japanese warlords, the ninja were often targeted and attacked. Ninjas eventually fought back, using their ability to disguise themselves in order to spy on the warlords and samurai. The intelligence they gathered allowed them to attack their enemies. These skills impressed the warlords, who decided to stop fighting the ninjas and hire them instead. Ninjas began to help warlords in their quest for power and land.

By practicing by the water, this ninja hopes to tap into the natural energy of the rocks and the stream.

Every move a ninja made was carefully calculated. It took years of discipline for a ninja to learn how to control every movement.

CHAPTER TWO

BECOMING A NINJA

A ninja would train as part of a larger group known as a clan. Each clan would have specific techniques and training methods, and the older members would teach the younger members the clan's secret techniques. At the peak of ninja activities, the cities of Koga and Iga housed about seventy ninja clans.

Jonin, Chunin, and Genin

Most clans had three classes of ninja. The ninja boss in a clan was called the *jonin*. He made the decision about who his ninjas would work for. Few ninjas knew who their jonin was because he used middlemen to deliver his orders. These middlemen were called *chunin*. Many chunin were also responsible for selecting the right ninja for the right job. The field agents were called the *genin*.

It is the genin's feats that have inspired many of the astonishing tales of the ninjas.

Early Ninja Training

Ninja training started at an early age. At about six years old, boys began playing games that required balance and quickness. They performed activities such as leaping over low bushes. As students got older, the training became more challenging. Students began to study striking and kicking techniques. Exercises that built strength were practiced until they could be done perfectly.

Ninjas even trained to move about in different ways so that they would not be easily seen. Learning how to use a small, stabbing step allowed the ninja to move silently through shallow water or dry leaves. Sideways walking helped a ninja move quietly in the shadows of buildings or in tight passages. A sweeping step was used to help a ninja move across wooden planks or straw matting.

Today, many try to replicate the training of the ninjas. Here is a demonstration of some of the techniques ninjas may have used.

A ninja also trained his mind. A well-trained ninja used his powers of concentration to perform amazing physical feats. For example, ninjas were trained to **dislocate** their shoulders from their sockets. This allowed them to escape after being captured and tied up by an enemy. Some ninjas were even able to dislocate their jaws. This prevented them from telling important information to a foe.

Staffs, Shurikens, and Other Weapons

Ninjas used a variety of weapons. One popular weapon was a wooden staff—a simple, yet deadly tool in a ninja's hands. A staff was usually three to six feet (one to two meters) long. Some ninja staffs were built to shoot poison-tipped darts.

Another popular weapon was the *shuriken*, or the hand-hidden blade. A shuriken is a sharp-edged metal blade that is thrown at an opponent. Shuriken can be round, square, or star-shaped.

A shuriken is one of the most well-known ninja weapons. This type of shuriken is often called a throwing star because of its shape.

The *shuko*, or climbing claws, were another favorite. Shuko are metal bands with several curved spikes on one side. A ninja would slip one over each of his hands and use the claws to climb trees or **scale** walls. Shuko could also be used as weapons to defend against a knife or a sword.

The *shinobi-zue*, or ninja cane, looked like an ordinary walking stick. However, it was hollowed out to hide a variety of fighting tools. Some canes contained hidden knives or metal chains. Some of them were even used as blowguns to shoot darts.

The swords used by ninjas were usually shorter than the heavy swords used by samurai. A lighter, smaller sword allowed a ninja to move quickly and to fight in small spaces. A ninja kept his sword in a **scabbard**, or holder. The scabbard was often longer than the sword. The ninja could use this extra space to hide secret papers, poisons, or other weapons. Some scabbards were made so that they could be used as breathing tubes. These scabbards had removable tips. When a ninja needed to hide underwater, he used his scabbard to breathe! He put one end of his scabbard in his mouth. The other end stuck out of the water, allowing him to get air.

GENIN'S TIP

Although most ninjas were male, there were also female ninjas. These ninjas were called *kunoichi*. Kunoichi were especially good as spies because most men did not expect women to be doing such dangerous work.

These actors reenact ninja fights at the Nikko Edo Village. Their short knives and fighting styles represent what real ninjas battles may have looked like.

Martial Arts

Ninjas were also masters of unarmed combat. This type of combat is called *taijutsu*. There are two different kinds of taijutsu.

One type of unarmed combat is called *dakentaijutsu* (dah-kehn-tye-jooht-sooh). This involves the art of strikes, blocks, and kicks. Strikes are usually made with the hand. They can also be made with the head, knee, elbow, or other body parts.

A second type of unarmed combat is *jutaijutsu*. This technique uses locks, holds, throws, and chokes. Jutaijutsu allowed a ninja to grab an opponent in a way that prevented escape. Ninjas also used their bodies to throw or flip opponents to the ground. This style of fighting allowed a smaller person to defeat a larger opponent.

Did Ninjas Use Magic?

Many myths claim that ninjas had magical powers. This claim is false. It was their special training and unusual way of fighting that often seemed magical to opponents.

Ninjas often used herbs and powders to produce effects that seemed magical. Some ninjas used special powders that stung the eyes. A ninja could throw this powder in an enemy's face. While the powder temporarily blinded the opponent, the ninja could run away. To his opponent, it seemed as if the ninja had disappeared into thin air!

Even before going on a mission, ninjas often cleverly planned their escape routes. This also contributed to the idea that the ninja had magical powers. Sometimes a ninja would dig a hole in the ground and hide there after the mission was completed. The ninja would jump into this hole and cover himself with dirt. People chasing him would think he had vanished.

Understanding and blending in with their natural surroundings was another way that ninjas seemed supernatural to others. For example, some ninjas could roll themselves up into balls. In the dark of night, they could look like large rocks on the ground. Their enemies would then be puzzled and frightened by the ninjas' sudden disappearance.

A Ninja's Home

Ninjas' homes looked like normal houses, but were often protected with booby traps and alarms.

Most ninjas' homes looked like average farmhouses. However, inside they were filled with secret passages and hidden spaces. Ninjas hid weapons and important documents in these secret places.

Some ninjas' homes even had entire hidden rooms built into them. Secret ladders and tunnels were also constructed in many ninja houses. Ninjas could use the ladders and tunnels to quickly escape an enemy.

Ninjas wanted to protect themselves at home from attackers and enemies, so they set up clever warning systems. They would string taut threads around the outside of their homes, and these threads would lead to warning bells inside their homes. Wherever someone approaching the house came in contact with the threads the bells would be activated. This warned the ninja that someone was coming.

Ninjas were often tasked by their masters with breaking into castles, like the Matsumoto Castle.

CHAPTER THREE

NINJA TECHNIQUES

Ninjas were known to use several different styles of attacks to trick and frustrate their opponents. Victory was the most important goal of a ninja, so they had no problem using methods that samurai, who preferred to fight face to face, would find dishonorable.

Attacking from the Inside

Ninjas often engaged in **siege** warfare. In siege warfare, an army surrounds a place such as a city or a castle to prevent supplies from reaching it. The army then waits for those inside to surrender.

A warlord's army would often lay siege to a castle after a small force of ninjas made a surprise attack. Ninjas would sneak into a castle at night and set fires. While the enemy was busy fighting the fires, the warlord's army attacked from outside. Surrounded by a warlord's soldiers and with ninjas prowling within the castle, the enemy usually surrendered.

Is this a monk or a ninja? Many ninjas would disguise themselves as monks or farmers so that they could spy on their enemies.

Shogun rulers, like those pictured above, would have to protect their secrets from ninja spies.

Spying was a skill used by many ninjas. A favorite technique was to slip into an enemy army camp to gather information. A ninja could disguise himself as a monk in order to move through the camp. Another might hide in tall grass outside a camp.

Once the ninja obtained the information he needed, he reported it to his commander. This information could include how many soldiers were in the camp or what types of weapons they had.

A ninja was sometimes required to change his entire lifestyle when he or she was on an assignment. Sometimes ninjas might have to take on a new identity and live in an enemy community. For example, a ninja might open a shop or become a farmer. Ninjas could live for months or even years among the enemy. During this time, they secretly gave information about the community to their commanders.

Ninjas would purposely pass on false information to the enemy. They would allow enemy agents to "discover" this so-called important information. Thinking the information they discovered was true, the enemy might take actions that would play into the hands of the ninja.

Some ninjas even acted as double agents. This meant that they pretended to be on the enemy's side when in fact the ninja was still loyal to his master.

GENIN'S TIP

The ninja art of stealth and espionage was known as *ninjutsu*.

Getting caught was a huge risk for ninja spies. Facing a trial, such as this one, would have been merciful compared to the torture that some spies endured.

A Gruesome Fate if Caught

Ninjas lived in constant danger. No matter how well trained or clever, a ninja was still at risk of being discovered. If a ninja was captured, he often faced a horrifying fate. Since he would not freely give up important information, his enemy would torture him. Among the tortures a ninja faced was having the skin stripped from his body. Another cruel torture was having all the bones in his body broken.

Some enemies would even boil a ninja alive in oil or water. Knowing these horrors awaited him, a ninja often took his own life if he could not escape capture.

Hired Killers

Sometimes warlords wanted to have their rivals killed, and they employed ninjas as **assassins**. While they were executing a lethal assignment, ninjas often used their training in stealth and cunning to carry out their deadly deed. Perhaps they would wait until their target was isolated—possibly traveling alone. Not having to eliminate additional protection or bodyguards would make the act of killing simpler. Ninjas would also blend in with their surroundings so they could use the element of surprise when attacking their enemy.

If necessary, ninjas could slip past bodyguards unnoticed to kill their target.

Oda Nobunaga was a skilled warrior and a strategic warlord.
He nearly succeeded in taking over all of Japan.

CHAPTER FOUR

THE DECLINE OF THE NINJAS

During the late 1500s, a single warlord began to take over and unify the power of all the Japanese warlords, ending the battles among the different factions. This new power structure greatly lessened the need for ninjas.

Iga's Ninjas Fall

Oda Nobunaga, a member of the Fujiwara family, was born in 1534. He became one of the most powerful warlords in Japan. During the 1570s and early 1580s, he and his forces waged many bloody battles.

Among Nobunaga's enemies were the ninjas. The exact reasons for this are not known. However, a tale tells of a day when Nobunaga was out hunting and his horse threw him. When Nobunaga landed on the ground, he felt he was being watched. He grew fearful, although he did not see anyone. He believed that there were ninjas nearby. He quickly rode away but he never forgot his fear of the ninjas. He decided to get rid of ninjas once and for all. Nobunaga and his army attacked Iga to destroy the ninjas there. Nobunaga's army won the battle. Most of Iga's ninjas were killed. From that time on, ninjas no longer lived or trained in Iga.

The Koga Ninjas and the Battle of Sekigahara

The Koga ninjas experienced a different fate. A warlord named Tokugawa Ieyasu hired a group of Koga ninjas to work for him. In 1600, the Koga ninjas fought in the Battle of Sekigahara. This was the largest battle ever fought in Japan. The ninjas engaged in siege warfare against opposing warlords. Ieyasu won the battle, allowing him to become shogun.

In about 1638, a group of farmers rebelled against their local leader because he treated them cruelly. Their revolt was called the Shimabara **Rebellion**. As the rebellion grew stronger, Ieyasu worried that it was a threat to his rule. He sent his

This is a small piece of a nineteenth century screen that depicts the Battle of Sekigahara, one of the most famous battles in history.

army and a group of ninjas to fight the farmers. The ninjas slipped into a castle called Hara and gathered information about how it was built. They learned where the enemy soldiers and the weapons were. Ninjas also stole food and supplies from the castle. Meanwhile, Ieyasu's army laid siege to the castle from outside its walls. The siege lasted for many weeks. Finally, the rebels inside Hara gave up. The rebellion was over.

No More Need for Ninjas

The Shimabara Rebellion was the last major battle in which ninjas played an important part. After 1638, Japan was at peace. Without a need for their military service, the ninjas' way of life was over. Instead, they became ordinary citizens. Over the years, many ninjas found jobs as farmers, tradesmen, teachers, policemen, or security agents. Some became outlaws or criminals. Finally, in 1868, all government-run ninja schools were closed. Several ninja masters continued to teach the old skills over the next few decades, but the days of the ninja warrior had come to an end.

The Shimabara Rebellion marked the end of the ninjas.

Kabuki theater combines singing, dancing, and mime. It is a beautiful art form that is popular throughout Japan.

The Ninja Legacy

As years passed, stories of the ninjas' strength and skill became part of Japanese culture. These stories often included fantastic elements such as the use of magical powers. In some stories, ninjas were able to turn themselves into animals. Other stories talked of ninjas as beings who could fly or disappear into thin air. Ninjas also appeared in **Kabuki**, a type of Japanese theater. Artists began to use ninjas and their fighting skills as inspiration for works of art. The ninja became an important and much loved figure, like a folk hero.

After World War II, Japanese moviemakers began using the legends and history of the ninjas in their films. This helped create a worldwide interest in the skills and accomplishments of Japan's ancient warriors. Ninja characters have appeared in hundreds of movies and TV shows. They are also frequently featured in video games, and are the heroes of countless books and comic books. Ninjas have even been the subject of children's cartoons, such as the *Teenage Mutant Ninja Turtles*, as well as video games, such as *Ninja Gaiden* and other franchises.

Ninjas will always have a place in the rich history of Japan, and will continue to live on in popular culture as well. People continue to be fascinated by their adept use of weapons and martial arts. While they have largely died out in real life, their legend is enduring.

GENIN'S TIP

Teenage Mutant Ninja Turtles began as a black-and-white comic book in the mid-1980s and remains popular with cartoon series, live-action films, and several lines of toys and action figures.

The Teenage Mutant Ninja Turtles are some of the most famous ninjas of all time.

GLOSSARY

assassins People who murder someone else, usually a politically important person; assassins are usually hired.

dislocate To move something out of its original place.

feudalism The medieval system in which people were given land and protection by the landowner, or lord, in return for working and fighting.

Kabuki A type of Japanese drama traditionally performed by men dressed in elaborate costumes.

lethal Harmful enough to kill.

martial arts Styles of fighting or self-defense that come mainly from the Far East.

ninja A person who is highly trained in ancient Japanese martial arts, especially one hired as a spy or assassin.

rebellion An armed fight against a government.

samurai A Japanese warrior who lived in medieval times.

scabbard A case that holds a sword, dagger, or bayonet when it is not in use.

scale To climb up something.

shogun The title given to the military leader of Japan from the twelfth to the nineteenth centuries.

siege The surrounding of a place, such as a city or a castle, to cut off supplies and then wait for those inside to surrender.

stealth To act in a secret and quiet manner.

technique A method or way of completing something that requires skill, as in the arts, sports, or sciences.

FIND OUT MORE

Books

Borda, Remigiusz, and Marian Winiecki. *The Illustrated Ninja Handbook: Hidden Techniques of Ninutsu*. North Clarendon, VT: Tuttle Publishing, 2014.

Cummins, Antony. *The Book of Ninja: The Bansenshukai—Japan's Premier Ninja Manual*. London, UK: Watkins Publishing, 2013.

Malam, John. *A Ninja Warrior! A Secret Job That's Your Destiny*. You Wouldn't Want to ... New York, NY: Franklin Watts, 2012.

Man, John. *Ninja: 1,000 Years of the Shadow Warrior*. New York, NY: William Morrow. 2013.

Yoda, Hiroko. *Ninja Attack! True Tales of Assassins, Samurai, and Outlaws*. North Clarendon, VT: Tuttle Publishing, 2013.

Websites

Encyclopedia Britannica's History of the Battle of Sekigahara

www.britannica.com/EBchecked/topic/533058/Battle-of-Sekigahara

Discover more about the historic battle that helped unite Japan and brought about the end of the ninja era. The page also has links to additional resources regarding the battle.

Japan-Guide.com's Official Sightseeing Guide to Ninjas

www.japan-guide.com/e/e2295.html

Learn more about ninjas, their history, and view photos of houses they built with trapdoors and secret passages.

The Ninja Museum of Igaryu

www.iganinja.jp/en/about/index.html

Take part in the "ninja experience." View photos and learn more about the shrine dedicated to the ancestor of the Abe clan, Obikonomikoto, and the foreign clans Shobikonanomikoto; Jodoshu temples; and the Chigachi Fortress Ruins.

INDEX